Contents

Chapter 1

The Scene as the Ice Age Began

The most recent time period of geologic history—the one we are still in—is called the Quaternary Period. The Quaternary has been a time mainly of ice. Through all but the last 10,000 years, it has been a time in which much of North America was uninhabitable, or not suitable for living.

Much of the landscape that we see every day was shaped by ice. The formation and movement of ice took place during the last 2 million years. Vast, flowing fields of ice called **glaciers** profoundly affected North America. Those glaciers eventually retreated northward to Greenland. Scientists do not yet know if they will move south again.

Prehistoric North America

When Ice Threatened Living Things

The Pleistocene

Jean F. Blashfield with Richard P. Jacobs

© 2006 Heinemann Library
a division of Reed Elsevier Inc.
Chicago, Illinois

Customer Service 888-454-2279
Visit our website at www.heinemannlibrary.com

Produced for Heinemann Library by Books Two, Inc.
Editorial: Jean Black, Deborah Grahame
Design: Michelle Lisseter
Illustrations: John T. Wallace, Top-Notch Productions
Picture Research: JLM Visuals
Production: Jean Black

Originated by Modern Age Repro
Printed and bound by South China Printing Company

10 09 08 07 06
10 9 8 7 6 5 4 3 2 1

Library of Congress Cataloging-in-Publication Data

Blashfield, Jean F.
  When ice threatened living things : the pleistocene / Jean F. Blashfield and Richard P. Jacobs.
    p. cm. -- (Prehistoric North America)
  Includes bibliographical references and index.
  ISBN 1-4034-7662-4
  1. Geology, Stratigraphic--Pleistocene--Juvenile literature. 2. Geology, Stratigraphic--Holocene--Juvenile literature. 3. Geology--North America--Juvenile literature. I. Jacobs, Richard P. II. Title. III. Series: Blashfield, Jean F. Prehistoric North America.
  QE697.B68 2005
  551.7'9--dc22

2004027620

Geology consultant: Marli Bryant Miller, Ph.D., University of Oregon
Maps: Ronald C, Blakey, Ph.D., Northern Arizona University
PICTURE CREDITS: COVER: Glacial meltwater, Charlie Crangle; Wooly mammoth skeleton, Breck P. Kent; TITLE PAGE: Musk oxen, US Fish & Wildlife Service
INTERIOR: Balkwell, David: 72 Archean; Crangle, Charlie: 73 Jurassic; The Field Museum: 46, 50 top, 51 top left, 54 top, 55 top, 55 bot, 59 top, 72 Cambrian, Silurian, Permian, 73 Paleocene, Miocene, Pliocene; Gilbert, Gordon R.: 48, 73 Eocene; Greenler, Robert: 4, 21; Harms, Carl: 34 bot; Heiman, Helga: 33 bot; Irving, Anthony: 23 ; Jacobs, Richard P.: 7, 11 bot, 15 top, 16, 18, 30 top, 30 bot, 32, 35 top, 35 bot, 36 top, 36 bot, 41 top, 41 bot, 49, 50 bot left, 50 bot right, 51 top right, 52, 53 top, 53 bot left, 53 bot right, 54 bot, 56 top, 59 bot, 63 top, ; Kent, Breck P.: 10 bot, 15 bot, 28, 34 top, 38 right, 45, 51 bot, 57, 58 bot, 62, 65 top, 65 bot, 72 Ordovician, Devonian, Mississippian, 73 Holocene; Laudon, Lowell R.: 5, 8 top, 68 top; Leszczynski, Zig: 73 Oligocene; Matthies, Michael:25; Miller, Marli: Page borders, 10 top, 11 top, 38 left, 40 top, 40 bot, 69, 73 Pleistocene; Minnich, John: 63 bot; NASA: 9, 24, 26, 27, 39, 43, 44; NPS: 17, 61; NOAA: 19, 20; Nicol, Keith: 67; Reblin, Michael: 37; Smithsonian National Museum of Natural History: 58 top, 72 Proterozoic, Pennsylvanian; USGS: 29, 60, 66 top, 66 mid, 66 bot, ; US Navy: 64; University of Michigan Exhibit Museum: 73 Triassic; Welford, M.W.: 8 bot; Zitzer, Marypat: 22, 33 top, 68 bot.

Some words are shown in bold, **like this**. You can find the definitions for these words in the glossary.

The End of the Cenozoic

The Cenozoic **Era** in geologic history began 65 million years ago. This is the time after the Age of Dinosaurs ended. The Cenozoic (meaning "recent life") is divided into two **periods**. The first period, called the Tertiary (meaning "third"), is by far the longest. It ended only 1.8 million years ago. The Quaternary (meaning "fourth") has, so far, lasted only 1.8 million years. It is the shortest time period in the **geologic time scale**.

Both the Tertiary and Quaternary are divided into smaller time periods called **epochs**. Most of the Quaternary Period—all but the last 10,000 years—is the Pleistocene Epoch. The Pleistocene is the Ice Age, though the name means "most recent." During the Pleistocene, continent-sized glaciers, called **ice sheets**, covered North America and northern Europe. The ice sheets spread out, then melted back, then spread out again. Such times of expanding ice are called **glaciations**. These may have occurred more than twenty times.

↳ *The ice sheets of the Ice Age have retreated to Greenland.*

The last 10,000 years is the epoch called the Holocene. This term means "completely recent." During the Holocene, living beings in North America—including humans—learned to live with the landscape left by the ice.

↰ *Antarctica's ice sheet represents the remains of the Pleistocene Ice Age.*

Scientists needed to determine when the Pleistocene started. Some thought it should be based on climate. Those scientists started with the beginning of the first major glaciation, which was 2.4 million years ago. Ultimately, scientists decided to separate the Quaternary from the Tertiary

PRECAMBRIAN TIME • *4.5 billion to 543 million years ago*
PALEOZOIC ERA • *543 to 248 million years ago*
MESOZOIC ERA • *248 to 65 million years ago*

CENOZOIC ERA • *65 million years ago to present*

Paleocene Epoch *65 to 54.8 million years ago*	Laramide orogeny Western Laurentia uplifted	Mammals and birds diversified First horse ancestors	
Eocene Epoch *54.8 to 33.7 million years ago*	Rockies uplifted Global cooling began	First mammals (whales) in sea First primates First cats and dogs	
Oligocene Epoch *33.7 to 23.8 million years ago*	North Atlantic opened Ice cap formed in Anatarctica	First apes Grasslands widespread	
Miocene Epoch *23.8 to 5.3 million years ago*	Columbia flood basalts	First human ancestors First mastodons	
Pliocene Epoch *5.3 to 1.8 million years ago*	Northern Hemisphere glaciation began Cascade Volcanoes	Large mammals abundant	
Pleistocene Epoch *1.8 million years ago to today*	Great glaciation of Northern Hemisphere	First modern humans Extinction of large mammals Humans entered North America	
Holocene *10,000 years ago to today*	Rifting continued in East Africa Human–caused global warming	Human-caused extinctions	

PHANEROZOIC TIME • 543 million years ago to present

CENOZOIC ERA • 65 million years ago to present

TERTIARY PERIOD • 65 to 1.8 million years ago

QUATERNARY PERIOD *1.8 million to today*

6

at 1.8 million years ago. This decision was based on a complex series of events that took place in the sea. It also took into account magnetic changes in the rock of Africa.

When the Pleistocene began 1.8 million years ago, the growth and movement of the first ice sheet had already begun. However, the other significant periods of glaciation all occurred within the Pleistocene. Therefore, when we talk about the "Ice Age," we are referring to the Pleistocene Epoch.

Farmers' fields in the Alps Mountains were limited in what they could produce because of the number of rocks found in the soil.

Discovery of the Ice Sheets

Glaciers once covered the northern parts of North America and Europe. This fact was not known until the 19th century. Farmers in Europe were used to discovering large boulders in their fields. These boulders were clearly not part of the soil they were plowing. The farmers were puzzled by the presence of the boulders. They just moved them or worked around them.

German-Swiss geologist Jean de Charpentier (1786–1855) collected legends in Switzerland about glaciers. People said the rivers of ice on the Alps Mountains had been much larger in the distant past. He wondered if those large glaciers could have moved the boulders. Then naturalist Louis Agassiz (1807–1873) explored the idea further. Perhaps glaciers had once covered Europe. These could have been so large that there had been no room for plant and animal life. Perhaps the ice had moved the boulders as well as the smaller rocks, pebbles, and soil around them. Agassiz wrote widely about the idea. He was just as widely scoffed at, however.

Gradually, geologists began to accept Agassiz's idea. At first, though, they thought there had been only one glacial period. They thought that period ended about 10,000 years ago. As they dug in the ground, however, they found **glacial** rock. This rock had layers without fossils alternating with layers containing **fossils**. Those fossils were of plants and animals that would have lived in warmer climates. Scientists gradually accepted the idea that Earth's Northern Hemisphere had been heavily glaciated at several times in the past with warm periods in between.

What is a Glacier?

Glaciers are rivers of ice. They consist of a special kind of ice that is denser and takes longer to melt than regular ice. They seem solid and motionless. However, glacial ice is capable of flowing downhill.

There are numerous glaciers on mountains today, all over the world. They even exist in mountain ranges near the equator. There, individual mountains are high enough to reach cold altitudes. In general, mountain glaciers are confined by the sides of valleys.

↳ *The typical mountain glacier is confined by the rock walls of a valley.*

Ice sheets are not confined. They are free to spread out across continents. The only ice sheets today are in Antarctica and Greenland. Usually a glacier must cover more than 19,300 square miles (50,000 sq km) to be called an ice sheet.

↰ *An ice sheet can cover a continent, gradually concealing rocks and even mountains beneath its dense ice.*

Glacial ice is ice that has been compacted over many centuries. It starts out as regular freezing water. It is in the form of six-sided ice crystals, or snow. Snow contains a great deal of air. When snow does not melt and more snow falls on top of it, some of the air is squeezed out. The crystals compact and melt slightly. They then refreeze as ice of a denser kind. Eventually, over thousands of years, the original snow has condensed to glacial ice. It contains very little air and is not easily melted.

In addition to air, glacial ice usually contains rock bits and other **sediments**. These make the ice heavier. Glaciers start to move because of their own weight. Gravity pulls them downward wherever the land slopes.

Glacial movement is also helped along by the fact that ice at the bottom of a traveling glacier may melt. The ice can then slide. Sometimes glaciers are in an extremely cold location. It may be so cold that there is no water at the base of it. Even so, such glaciers move because of changes that occur within the ice. This is similar to the internal changes that take place in a bowl of Jell-O that is sitting on an inclined surface.

In general, glaciers flow between 33 and 1,000 feet (10 to 300 m) a year. The speed depends on the slope of the ground and whether or not there is water underneath. One glacier in Greenland is the fastest-moving one on Earth. It moves 4.5 miles (7 km) a year.

Greenland's Glaciers

Greenland is the world's largest island. It has both an ice sheet and individual glaciers. These spread out around the ice sheet's fringe. The ice in the Arctic Ocean around Greenland is not glacial ice. It is regular ice that is free to float and break up. It often melts in summer. Floating within that Arctic ice, though, may be **icebergs**. These are chunks of glacial ice that have broken off Greenland's glaciers. Icebergs can float around in the ocean for years before melting completely.

↻ *A small glacier may form in a basin on the side of a mountain not reached by direct sun.*

A glacier can be as small as the permanent ice in a small mountainside basin never reached by sunshine. It can be as large as the ice sheet across an entire continent. Glaciers can grow by the accumulation of new snow. They can also shrink by **evaporation** at the surface or by **calving**. A glacier calves when the lower end of it reaches the edge of the land it's on. Its weight makes it break. It then falls into the sea as an iceberg. Icebergs float with most of their structure under water. This is because the ice is almost as dense as water.

It seems as though glacial ice is hard and very tough. But ice that is deep within a glacier is underneath hundreds of feet of other ice. As a result, it is under a lot of pressure. Given time, this pressurized ice can be described as "weak." Such ice spreads out like thick syrup being poured upon the landscape. It will flow wherever there is a low spot for it to go.

A glacier begins to retreat, or melt back, when the climate warms enough. The toe, or **leading edge**, of the glacier melts faster than new ice can be added at the top.

↩ A glacier calves when a section breaks off the front of the glacier at the edge of land. The resulting iceberg can float in the ocean for years.

An Active Glacier

Athabasca Glacier is found in Jasper National Park of the Canadian Rockies. It is easily reached by a short walk from Icefield Parkway. This road runs past many other glaciers in the park.

In front of the leading edge, or toe, of the glacier are deposits of rock material. These deposits indicate that at present the glacier is retreating. The ice itself still flows

↖ The leading edge of Athabasca Glacier

forward. However, the position of the leading edge of the glacier is retreating. Therefore, the ice must be melting at a faster rate than it can flow forward. Years earlier, the forward flow of ice exceeded its rate of melting. As a result, the leading edge advanced. The glacier's retreat leaves deposits of rock behind.

Anyone walking on the glacier can see large cracks, or **crevasses**, unless they are covered with new snow. Crevasses form in the top layer of a glacier. This is because the top gets brittle while the bottom is more plastic as it moves forward. Tension between the two kinds of ice makes the brittle top layer crack.

↩ A crevasse

Crevasses on big glaciers can be dangerous if they are covered with snow. Mountaineers usually "rope up" when they hike across glaciers. This is because of the possibility of encountering hidden crevasses. If one of the climbers falls into a crevasse, the others can stop the fall by digging into the glacier with their ice axes. Then they can

11

The Cooling Climate

At the end of the Tertiary Period, glaciation of the Northern Hemisphere was already underway. Then, starting more than 3 million years ago, the planet's temperature dropped even more. This happened quite quickly. Earth functions within a fairly narrow temperature range. It takes a drop in average temperature of only about 7 to 10 degrees Fahrenheit (4 or 5 degrees Centigrade) for an ice age to begin.

The already cooling climate made changes in the shape of North America. It looked different than it had 10 million years before. It was different than it would look again until about 10,000 years ago.

As the climate cooled, Earth's water became bound up in ice. The level of the sea went down as much as 330 feet (100 m). The **continental shelves** were exposed. Continental shelves are the areas of land that gradually slope downward into the sea from continental land.

The exposure of the continental shelves made the continent considerably larger than it had been before. This was the case especially in the east. The low-lying **Coastal Plain** around the Gulf of Mexico expanded into the gulf, all the way down into Mexico. The continental shelves in the warmer regions became ordinary land. The land was populated with forests and other vegetation. Land animals expanded into the new habitat.

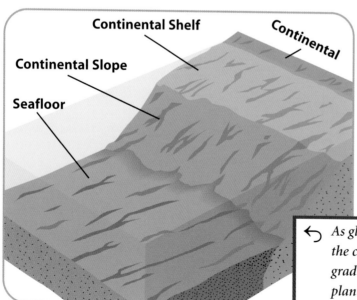

Continental Shelf

Continental

Continental Slope

Seafloor

↰ *As glaciers formed, sea level dropped, exposing the continental shelves. This new land gradually turned into regular habitat for plants and animals.*

LOW LAND

UPLANDS

MOUNTAINS

VERY
SHALLOW SEA

SHALLOW
SEA

DEEP SEA

TRENCH

MODERN
BORDERS

N

This map shows North America as it was 2 million years ago, just before the Pleistocene started. The very light blue color shows continental shelf that would later be exposed as the level of the sea fell. The area at the top left would become Beringia, the wide land bridge connecting Asia and North America.

One of the most significant continental shelves that was exposed has been called the Bering land bridge, or Beringia. This was no narrow bridgelike strip of land, as we sometimes think today. Instead, it was a vast land that connected Asia and North America. It stretched from the Aleutian Islands in the south almost to the North Pole.

Beringia came to be occupied by many animals. These moved from Asia in the search for new habitat. Other animals moved from North America for the same reason. For almost 2 million years, the Bering land bridge was exposed during glacial periods. It was submerged in the ocean during **interglacial** periods.

The land called Beringia was a subcontinent connecting Asia and North America during the Ice Age. The darker brown color is today's land.

What was North America Like?

Some areas of Wisconsin and Minnesota were left exposed when the glaciers surrounded them. From these areas, we can tell a little bit about what the surface landscape of central Canada and the northern United States was like before the first glaciation. The old landscape can also sometimes be reconstructed by digging down through all the rock and soil moved by the ice. Basically, though, the landscape was destroyed and rebuilt by ice time after time.

Glaciers are the most powerful natural agent known for rearranging the land. Sediments are scraped off and moved around by glacial action. Glacial action in North America gives us important information about the original rock of the continent, called the **craton**. It has been estimated that a layer of **sedimentary rock** 100 feet (33 m) thick was scraped off the craton in northern Canada. This scraping was caused by the moving ice during the last glaciation.

↵ Fumaroles along the Firehole River in Yellowstone

Yellowstone, a Pleistocene Caldera

Yellowstone National Park is an area where heat from inside the earth is clearly at work. There is a **hot spot** in the mantle beneath the area. In the past, volcanoes have formed over this hot spot. Even today, the heat is responsible for the many hot springs, mud volcanoes, **fumaroles** (steam vents), **geysers**, and other heat features found in the park.

Starting about 2 million years ago, numerous volcanoes formed in the region, with major eruptions occurring. The first one, called Huckleberry Ridge, may have been the largest eruption ever to have occurred on Earth.

The last cycle of volcanism took place about 600,000 years ago. In one large volcano the lava chamber in the **lithosphere** emptied out, and the volcanic rock above it collapsed. The collapse formed a basin, called a **caldera**. It is almost 1,000 square miles (2,600 sq km) in area. The central area of Yellowstone National Park exists within this caldera. The heat plume is still active under the park. Some scientists think that volcanism in Yellowstone may start again in the future.

Gibbon Falls flows over part of the caldera rim. ↵

Other processes that make and remake Earth continued during the Pleistocene. The contact between the North American **tectonic plate** and the Pacific plate caused many earthquakes. Volcanoes continued to rise in the Cascade Range of Washington State and British Columbia and in the southwest.

The land was flooded time and again. This occurred away from the glacial areas in the north. Plentiful rain fell because of cooler temperatures. This was the case even in areas that were usually desert. When rains fell, rivers flowed. They carried sediment to the ocean. The exposed continental shelves were built up by sedimentation. The beautiful beaches of southeastern United States may have been created by sediment carried from the ice sheets.

Sediments from farther north were ground to tiny grains and carried by rivers to the southeast. Today, such beaches as this one in North Carolina are tourist destinations.

The ice sheets did not expand into the southern and western region. These regions are where large mammals that had developed during the Tertiary Period continued to live. Mammoths, saber-toothed cats, and giant armadillos inhabited ice-free regions. Horses and camels grazed southern grasslands. All of these animals had disappeared by the end of the Pleistocene.

The entire Quaternary Period has been a time of great change in North America. But the kinds of changes have been very different from those that occurred in earlier geologic times. First there would be almost 2 million years of ice and its effects. Then it was time for human beings to create more profound changes on the continent.

A Late Pleistocene Cinder Cone

In the grasslands of northern New Mexico stands Mount Capulin. This volcano erupted about 60,000 years ago. It is a type of volcano called a cinder cone. From the base, it can be seen to be almost perfectly cone-shaped. A road runs up and around this cinder cone. Eventually, the road reaches a parking area on the rim of its **crater**.

The cone is composed of dark-colored ash and cinder. These fell around the central crater after erupting from it. No lava flowed from the central crater. However, some flows did occur from secondary vents, or openings, at the base of the cone.

From the rim, paved foot trails lead down into the crater. This rim is about 1,000 feet (330 m) above the surrounding area. Viewpoints are found along another trail that follows the crater's rim. These trails have been paved because walking on the steep slopes of loose cinder is very difficult.

Chapter 2

Cycles in Earth and Ice

During the Pleistocene, ice sheets covered much of North America. These grew, retreated, grew again, and retreated again. Louis Agassiz and his colleagues in the 19th century assumed that there had been only one glacial period. Geologists in the 20th century decided otherwise. They analyzed different layers of sedimentary rock and the fossils contained in them. They determined that there had been four glacial periods in North America and five in Europe. In between the glacial episodes were warmer periods, or interglacials. Today, we are probably in an interglacial.

Today, geologists recognize that there were even more than four or five glacial periods. Indeed, there were many more. They learned this by analyzing samples of the seafloor. Different layers of the seafloor showed which kinds of microscopic fossil plants and animals (**plankton**) lived at different times. The species that thrived and left their **calcium carbonate** shells behind changed with water temperature. Geologists have identified at least twenty, perhaps as many as thirty, glacial periods by studying fossil plankton.

Divers taking seafloor samples to study how climate has changed

Many people still use four traditional glacial periods for the last 2 million years in North America. They were named for the location of rocks studied to analyze the movement and duration of ice sheets. From the earliest to the latest, they are called Nebraskan, Kansan, Illinoian, and Wisconsinan.

Oddly enough, eastern Asia was not glaciated. This was probably because the climate of the region was too dry to make enough snow.

Regular snow and glacial ice high in the Alps Mountains

HOW DO THEY KNOW
There Were Many Glaciations?

Scientists study the **isotopes** of oxygen found in shells on the seafloor to identify glacial periods. Isotopes are varieties of a chemical element that differ in the number of neutrons (particles without a charge) in the nucleus of the atom. In seawater, the element oxygen may have 16 neutrons or it may have 18. The ratio of O-16 to O-18 available at any one time depends on the temperature of the water.

Single-celled animals such as **foraminiferans** and single-celled plants such as **coccoliths** make shells out of calcium carbonate. They do this by using oxygen in the ocean water. That shell material contains oxygen of the isotope variety available at the time they lived. Their shells accumulated on the ocean floor when they died. Scientists taking **core** samples, such as the one at the right, can analyze the different layers of material. They calculate what the temperature of the sea was at the time the layers were laid down.

During cooler times, proportionately more O-18 is incorporated into the shells than during warmer times. Cooler times existed when large ice sheets covered much of the continents. Later, the planet's temperature warmed during an interglacial. As a result, the ratio of O-16 to O-18 increased in the seawater and, as a result, in the shells of the creatures living at the time.

Analysis of the seafloor layers changed a lot of thinking about glacial periods. During the first million years of the Pleistocene, the individual glaciations occurred frequently. Each produced about the same amount of ice. Because of this, geologists have decided that the earlier Nebraskan and Kansan periods do not stand out the way the two later glacial periods do.

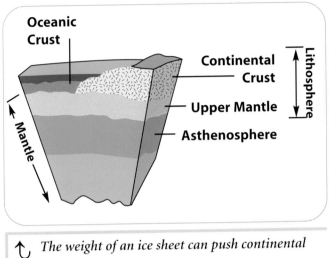

Oceanic Crust

Continental Crust

Upper Mantle

Asthenosphere

Lithosphere

Mantle

The weight of an ice sheet can push continental crust down into the asthenosphere.

A Glaciation

At some point, the temperature of the planet cooled enough so that not all of a winter's snow melted by the end of summer. Glaciers started to form. Once glaciers existed, they formed even faster because ice reflects the sun's heat back into space. If solar heat is reflected instead of absorbed, the planet's surface fails to get warmer in the summer.

The ice sheets that covered so much of North America were probably about 10,000 feet (3 km) thick. That is about the same thickness as today's ice sheets in Antarctica and Greenland. Their sheer weight probably depressed the continental crust into the **asthenosphere** as much as 1,000 feet (300 m). The asthenosphere is the upper part of Earth's **mantle**. There, some of the rock is **molten**, or liquefied by heat. As the ice sheet melted back, the crust gradually rose again. In some places it is still rising.

This ice block has broken off a thin edge of the huge ice sheet covering Antarctica.

↰ *The Arctic **tundra** is ground that is permanently frozen beneath the surface. Only in summer does the topsoil thaw and support some plant life.*

On the edges of the ice sheets, deeper ground was permanently frozen. This is still true in the Arctic today. A band of **permafrost**, or permanently frozen subsoil, extended across central North America. The air temperature there was considerably colder than we know today. The average temperature was probably below 21°F (–6°C). Today, it is about 52°F (11°C).

Earth Factors in the Glaciations

Much of the planet has been covered with ice at various times during the Quaternary. There are many reasons for this. Scientists don't know yet which of the reasons is most important, or how they affect each other.

The position of the continents on Earth is an important factor. Vast ice sheets do not form over ocean water. The largest continents moved into the Northern Hemisphere. This happened after the breakup of the **supercontinent** known as **Pangea**. There was thus more land in the north for ice sheets to form on. A previous glacial period occurred in the late Paleozoic Era, about 250 million years ago. During this time, a great deal of land was near the South Pole. The primary ice sheets were in the south.

Antarctica separated from Australia about 30 million years ago. At the same time, an ocean current began to form around the polar continent. However, it was not fully established until about 3 million years ago.

This powerful current formed a "fence." Even today this fence keeps warmer water from reaching the icy continent. The bigger ice sheet built up on Antarctica. Its lower temperature contributed to the cooling of the whole planet.

Also about 3 million years ago, the Isthmus of Panama closed. North America and South America were now attached to each other. This new land served as another "fence." It prevented warm water in the Caribbean region from entering the Pacific Ocean. Instead, the warm water formed a new ocean current, the Gulf Stream. The Gulf Stream carries warm water northward past the United States. Then it flows eastward where it warms western Europe.

This change in ocean circulation made more snow fall over the Arctic region than had previously fallen. When more snow falls in winter than can melt in the summer, some of it stays permanently in place. The following winter, more snow falls on top of the remaining snow from the previous year. The old snow underneath begins to compact. A glacier has begun.

What about Volcanoes?

Some scientists think that the amount of volcanic ash and gases in the atmosphere can also contribute to the cooling of the planet. Such materials in the air block the sunlight from reaching the surface. One example these scientists use is the period from about 1450 to 1850. This period is often called the Little Ice Age. Volcanic activity increased abruptly and global temperatures went down. The Vikings had been living in Greenland for several hundred years. They abandoned their homes and returned to Europe. But even in Europe, the growing season was often too short for crops to grow. People starved as a result.

Another factor was the amount of carbon dioxide in the atmosphere. Carbon dioxide is a gas that holds the sun's heat in the atmosphere. There may have been a reduced amount of carbon dioxide in the atmosphere during the past 3 million years. The amount of carbon dioxide can vary with the amount of plant life. (Remember—plants take in carbon dioxide and give off oxygen.) At times, there can be an abundance of plant life—either in the ocean or on land. As a result, the amount of carbon dioxide in the atmosphere is reduced. The temperature can go down. But the question remains: What makes the amount of plant life vary?

Those Earth factors, however, don't explain why there were so many periods during which ice sheets grew and then melted back. This situation probably has more to do with astronomical factors.

Astronomical Factors

We tend to think that Earth's movement in the solar system is one of the unchanging facts of the universe. But that's not so. In 1920, a Serbian climate specialist, Milutin Milankovitch (1879–1958), suggested ways that Earth's basic temperature can be affected. These ways include changes in Earth's **orbit** and in the tilt of the planet on its **axis** as it moves around in its orbit. He found that these astronomical factors occurred in repeating patterns, or cycles.

The tilt of Earth in its orbit is the reason our planet has seasons. If Earth's axis were perpendicular (vertical, or straight up and down) to the plane of the planet's orbit, there would be no seasons because the sun's rays would strike Earth the same all the time. But there is a tilt, so there are seasons on Earth.

The tilt of the axis changes slightly over a long period of time. It moves back and forth between a tilt of 22 degrees and one of 25 degrees. The time period of this cycle is about 41,000 years.

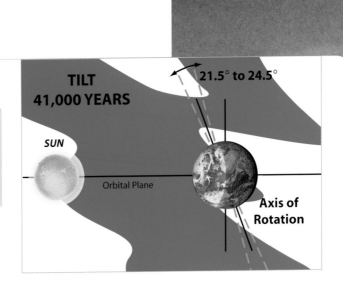

**TILT
41,000 YEARS**

21.5° to 24.5°

SUN

Orbital Plane

**Axis of
Rotation**

*One factor that may affect the
buildup of ice is the tilt of
Earth's axis. It changes slightly
in a cycle that lasts 41,000 years.*

Another cycle is called **precession**. Earth wobbles in its orbit. As a result, sometimes the axis points to Polaris (the North Star) and sometimes to another star. This wobble occurs in a cycle lasting 23,000 years.

A third cycle described by Milankovitch is the changing shape of Earth's orbit. He found that the orbit changes from nearly circular to less circular and back again. This cycle lasts 100,000 years.

During the Cenozoic Era, the cycles he described were all overlapping and affecting each other. Together, these factors kept sunshine from warming Earth. The planet was already somewhat cooler because of Earth factors. These astronomical factors may have created the finishing touch on a glacial world.

In the 1990s, scientists realized that another astronomical factor might have played a role in the formation of glaciers. It has to do with the amount of cloud in the atmosphere.

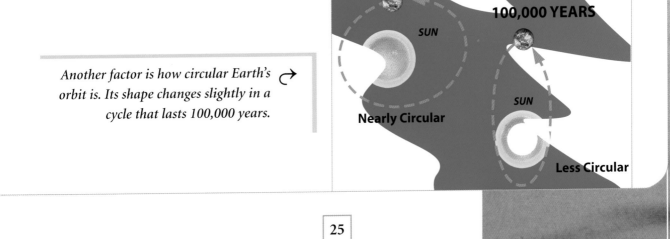

**ORBITAL SHAPE
100,000 YEARS**

SUN

Nearly Circular

SUN

Less Circular

*Another factor is how circular Earth's
orbit is. Its shape changes slightly in a
cycle that lasts 100,000 years.*

The scientists found that, in addition to Earth's orbit changing shape, it also changes position a little bit. It changes enough so that every 100,000 years, the planet goes through a ring of dust. This ring orbits the sun in a plane similar to that of the planet Jupiter. Earth doesn't accumulate very much dust when it passes through the dust. Perhaps, however, it's enough to influence the planet's climate. The dust increases the clouds in the atmosphere, blocking the sun.

↰ *Thick, low-lying clouds such as these can prevent warming sunlight from reaching the planet's surface.*

Rapid Changes in Climate

All these factors worked together. They created a 2-million-year period of many glaciations and retreats. The glaciations occurred when the Northern Hemisphere was not getting as much direct sunlight as it does in the warmer periods.

A step-by-step procedure of how ice sheets form and then melt has been proposed. Remember, though, that there are many complexities that are not included here.

NASA scientists have proposed that Mars, too, had an ice age, probably from 2.1 million to 400,000 years ago. The tilt of its axis and dust in its thin atmosphere may have led to a buildup of ice at the poles. This NASA artwork shows how Mars might have looked.

1. Northern Canada was ice-free. As a result, the land did not have extra weight on it. That part of the continental crust stood high in the asthenosphere. The temperature of the planet was going down. The most elevated part of continent—northern Canada—collected snow. This snow did not melt in summer. There was a lot of snow because the Gulf Stream carried so much moisture as it traveled northward. Ice built up, gradually turning to glacial ice. This ice spread out from the starting point of the glaciation near Hudson Bay.

2. The ice sheet continued to get thicker and spread out more. Eventually it became quite heavy. As a result, the continent started to sink into the asthenosphere again. At the same time, the temperature of the Northern Hemisphere had become extremely cold. The ocean froze, as a result. The warmth of the Gulf Stream could no longer make ocean water evaporate. Snow stopped falling in such large amounts. The ice sheet began to melt faster than new ice could accumulate. The ice sheet was in retreat.

3. With less ice sheet, the sun's rays could warm more of the continent. As a result, temperatures rose. That made the glacial ice melt even faster. Also, the ocean ice melted. Evaporation could again take place. The precipitation was then rain instead of snow. This made the ice sheet melt even faster. The Northern Hemisphere had entered an interglacial period.

4. The weight of the ice sheet left the continent. Meanwhile, the crust was free to rise again if astronomical conditions were right. The whole cycle started all over.

Chapter 3

The Last Glaciation: Shaping Today's Land

Geologists know that ice sheets came out of the north many times. The glacial ice spread as far south as Nebraska, Kansas, Illinois, and Wisconsin. The scientists found rock that was piled up by the glaciers. They also found scratches and gouges made by the moving ice. However, they don't know much about what the moving ice sheets did to the land during the early glaciations. These took place before the last glaciation started about 100,000 years ago. That last glaciation was the Wisconsinan. It is the one that turned much of North America into the land we know now. It was probably typical of earlier glaciations.

Scientists know that the Wisconsinan was not a single event. Instead, over the last 100,000 years there were two spikes in glaciation. There was a brief warm spell in between. Two ice sheets were forming and retreating. As a result, the Wisconsinan churned up the surface of northern North America.

↰ *Glacial striations on rock show which way the glacier moved.*

Moving Rock

A moving glacier can pick up loose material, which it then incorporates into the ice. If it picks up a lot of sand, a glacier polishes any rock it moves over. If it picks up larger rocks and carries them along, it can make sharp, straight lines in the surface rock it travels over. These marks, called striations, are visible centuries later. They are evidence that a glacier has passed that way. Geologists can determine where different ice sheets started by mapping the striations on rock.

↰ *A mountain goat surveys a glacial valley formed during the Wisconsinan glacier.*

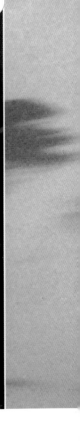

Scouring by a Glacier

Evidence of glacial **scouring** is seen everywhere in Maine's Acadia National Park. The park area is located on islands off the rocky coast. The continental glacier once covered it. As the ice slowly flowed, it removed soil that had covered the **granite** and other hard **igneous rock**. The **bedrock** has been heavily polished and grooved by materials in the ice.

↳ Scoured rock

The moving ice shaped elongated bedrock hills. It gently smoothed the side that faced the flow of ice. The bedrock on the downstream side of the hills was plucked loose by the ice. This caused that side to be steeper and more jagged. Some people think the shape produced looks like a sheep (below).

A sheep-shaped hill of bedrock, left by glacial action ↪

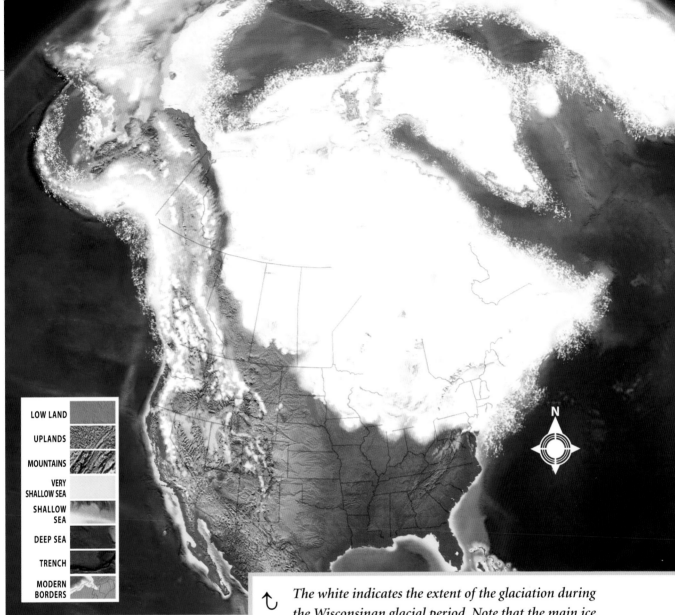

LOW LAND	
UPLANDS	
MOUNTAINS	
VERY SHALLOW SEA	
SHALLOW SEA	
DEEP SEA	
TRENCH	
MODERN BORDERS	

The white indicates the extent of the glaciation during the Wisconsinan glacial period. Note that the main ice sheet and the western Cordilleran do not quite meet.

The Wisconsinan's largest ice sheet is called the Laurentide. It started in northeastern Canada in the region that is now Hudson Bay. From there, it flowed outward in all directions. In the west, it met the Keewatin ice sheet. This had started in northwestern Canada. Together, they flowed down into the United States. A separate ice sheet is called the Cordilleran. This one spread out from the Canadian Rockies. It covered the western part of Canada and part of Alaska. These ice sheets were thickest at their starting point, about 10,000 feet (3,000 m) deep.

Rock moved by an ice sheet is not just a boulder here and some sand there. An ice sheet can pick up and carry with it incredible quantities of sedimentary rock as it moves.

The Laurentide ice sheet changed the face of northern North America. This ice sheet spread outward from Hudson Bay. As it spread, it scoured the land down to the original bedrock of the continent's craton. That exposed craton is the **Canadian Shield**. The Canadian Shield has only a thin layer of soil on it. It is much too thin to be useful as agricultural land. This makes it unlike the rest of Canada and the glaciated part of the United States.

The rock and soil scraped off the Canadian Shield ended up elsewhere. The glacial ice carried it along. Eventually, the ice sheet stopped moving and started melting back. Then the ice dropped all this unsorted rock and soil and left it behind. This material is called **glacial till**.

The Canadian Shield is the area of the craton that was scraped clean of sedimentary rock by glaciations. Compare this map with the one on the previous page. The Shield matches the shape of the main ice sheet. The green section is the craton that was not scraped clean.

Huge quantities of glacial till, such as the rocks, pebbles, and soil in Alberta, Canada, shown here, were deposited by the glaciations.

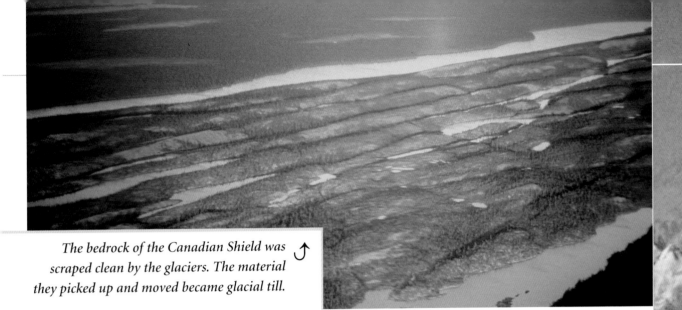

The bedrock of the Canadian Shield was scraped clean by the glaciers. The material they picked up and moved became glacial till. ↰

Glacial till was deposited from southern Illinois eastward through New York. It was also spread northwest through Alberta all the way up to the Arctic Ocean. This deposited glacial till was spread fairly flat. It left the Great Plains as huge productive lands that became prairies. Today, these same lands are used for agriculture.

Moraines

Picked-up material can also work its way down through the ice and fall out the bottom of the glacier as it moves. Any collection of such material is called a **moraine**. A moving glacier leaves a ridge of rocky debris along its side. Such debris is called a lateral moraine. (*Lateral* means "side.")

This hiker in Switzerland stands on a lateral moraine, the rocky debris left at the side of a glacier as it moved through a valley in the mountains. ↱

↰ *An end moraine builds up at the point where a glacier stops moving forward and begins to retreat. End moraines can be small or cover part of a continent.*

The rocky debris can also be carried to the end of the glacier. This is the area where it melts. Even if the glacier doesn't keep moving forward, the internal ice keeps flowing. The debris continually falls out of the ice. It accumulates in a pile, called an end moraine.

An area may have several end moraines. This is because glaciers can stop moving for a while for a number of reasons. The end moraine farthest from the beginning of the ice sheet is called a terminal moraine.

Moraines can be huge. New York's Long Island and Massachusetts's Cape Cod are part of a terminal moraine. Between the two structures, there are signs of the same terminal moraine in southern Connecticut and Rhode Island.

The ice sheet also left small structures marking the landscape. **Drumlins** are long, narrow hills of glacial till. The name *drumlin* is from an ancient Gaelic word for "hill." Often nearby are **kettle** holes. Kettles formed when a chunk of the glacier broke off. Before melting, it was covered by glacial till. Eventually, the chunk melted and the till sank, leaving a circular depression in the ground.

↰ *Kettles are holes left in the land after glacial chunks have melted. Many kettles like those in the photo are visible from the air.*

↖ Drumlin swarm in a lake

Drumlins — Streamlined Hills

Drumlins are common to areas that were once covered by continental glaciers. They are smooth, elongated hills. They are usually composed of loose rock material. Farmers often have to follow the shape of a drumlin when they plow. The length of a drumlin is in the same direction that the glacial ice once flowed.

Most drumlins are steep on one end. They are gently sloping on the other, away from the source of the ice. The steeper end usually faces the direction from which the ice flowed, or "upstream." Perhaps the more streamlined drumlins were shaped by faster moving ice, while more rounded ones were shaped by slower moving ice.

Some areas in North America contain large concentrations of drumlins. These are called drumlin swarms. A drumlin swarm in New York includes over 10,000 of these streamlined hills.

↩ Roads passing through drumlin swarms go up and down while passing over the drumlins.

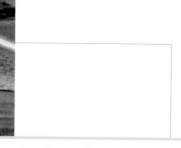

↰ *An esker makes a snakelike barrier across Wisconsin farmland.*

Meltwater sometimes formed tunnels in the ice where it touched the ground at the bottom of the glacier. Sand and other sediments filled those tunnels. Then, when the ice sheet melted away, snakelike ridges called **eskers** were left behind. The sediment forming an esker is composed of rounded gravel. This was sorted by particle size as it was carried by running water.

The Ice Age Trail

Moraines are evident as visitors pass along the Ice Age National Scenic Trail in Wisconsin. These moraines mark the glaciers that formed during the last glaciation. Drumlins and kettle holes, as well as mounded glacial till like that to the left, are common sights along the trail. Wisconsin is home to 15,000 lakes. Most of them are in depressions dug out by the glaciers.

The trail has been in the planning stage since 1958. It currently covers about 300 miles (483 km). When completed, it may be 1,200 miles (1,930 km) long.

A section of southwestern Wisconsin was circled by ice during the Wisconsinan but never touched. It is called the Driftless Area. *Drift* is another work for glacial till.

Glaciers and Valleys

Valleys, or low-lying areas, between mountains often contain rivers. Over the centuries, the river can cut its way down through the rock, making a V-shaped landform like the one at the right.

Today, if you see a V-shaped valley, you know that it probably never had a glacier running through it. This is because glaciers typically form U-shaped valleys. As the glacier develops, it expands to the side and begins to flow. It both scrapes rock from each side and pulls in rocks as it moves. The result is a U instead of a V.

This V-shaped valley was created by the erosion of rock by the river. It has never had a glacier in it. ↪

The ice sheet did not reach many of the mountains in the North American west. However, they frequently have U-shaped valleys. These valleys were dug out by their own individual glaciers.

During the Wisconsinan ice sheet, individual glaciers made their way through mountain valleys to the sea. These were spawned by the ice sheets. They cut deeply into the rock. When the glaciers melted, these typical U-shaped valleys with steep sides filled with water. Today, they are **fjords** (pronounced FYORDZ). The most famous fjords are in Norway and Greenland. Other, usually smaller fjords are found in British Columbia and in southeastern Canada.

Yosemite's U-shaped Valleys

During the Ice Age, California's Yosemite Valley was shaped by glacial ice. A large glacier moved through the valley. Smaller **tributary** glaciers fed this large glacier. (A tributary is a stream that flows to a larger stream or other body of water. Therefore, a tributary glacier flows to and feeds a larger glacier.) Its present steep-sided U-shape is typical of valleys carved by glaciers. This is in contrast to the V-shape of valleys shaped by rivers.

↰ The U-shaped Yosemite Valley

↲ A hanging valley in Yosemite

In Yosemite, smaller U-shaped valleys hang above the large, main glacial valley. These smaller valleys indicate the paths taken by tributary glaciers. Streams now flow through many of the hanging valleys. They become waterfalls when they meet the much deeper main valley.

Where Does All That Water Go?

As the Wisconsinan ice sheet melted back, about 90 percent of the land it had covered became lakes. The glacier had gouged out depressions in the land. These filled with meltwater. There were thousands of lakes. Some of them remain today. Others, however, were encased in basins of sediment. The sediment later eroded away, releasing the water in the lakes.

Wood Buffalo National Park is Canada's largest national park. It was established to protect bison and whooping cranes. The park is a huge maze of marshes, streams, ponds, and bogs. These were left by the melting of the last ice sheet because the flat land does not drain well.

In New York, the ice sheet left a series of more distinct lakes. These are called the Finger Lakes. They are a series of long, narrow lakes that appear to be lined up north to south. It seems as if they are fingers coming from an invisible hand. Rock formed in the Devonian Period was scraped clean by the ice sheet. The lakes were gouged out of the channels of northward-flowing rivers. There are moraines piled up at the southern end of each lake.

New York's Finger Lakes were gouged out of the rock by the Wisconsinan glaciation. They are seen here from space in winter. ↱

↰ *After the waters of Glacial Lake Missoula broke free from an ice dam, later flooding scoured and eroded the area called the Channeled Scablands in Washington State.*

Ancient Lakes

A huge lake was created when a 2,000-foot (610 m)-thick finger of the Cordilleran ice sheet trapped the flow of the Columbia River in northern Idaho. This made the flow back up. The huge lake that formed is called Glacial Lake Missoula. It lasted several thousand years. Eventually, the wall of ice gave way. Ancient shorelines from this lake can be seen high on the hills behind the University of Montana campus in Missoula, Montana.

This kind of backed-up glacial lake was fairly common. What wasn't so common was what happened when the ice dam making Lake Missoula burst. About 17,000 years ago, a wall of water exploded downstream. This wall is thought to have been 2,000 feet (610 m) high. The power of the water chiseled canyons in the walls. It rushed over a cliff, making a waterfall that was more than 3 miles (4.8 km) across. It had a drop of 400 feet (122 m). That cliff is now called Dry Falls.

The Channeled Scablands seen from above. The smooth areas are where meltwater rushed between mountains and scoured the land. ↱

↑ Dry Falls (the cliffs in the background) stretches more than 3 miles (4.8 km) in eastern Washington.

Changing Water Levels

Continental glaciers had stored water in the form of ice. When the continental glaciers were melting, the resulting meltwater formed many rivers and lakes. Also, sea level rose. Today, there is no new meltwater available. As a result, most rivers and lakes have disappeared or have shrunk greatly. Evidence of these changing water levels is found throughout much of North America.

At Dry Falls in the state of Washington, glacial meltwater once roared over a waterfall many times greater than Niagara Falls. Only a long cliff and the remains of large water-carved pools beneath the cliff can be seen today.

Looking up from a dry basin, terraces are seen along the sides of mountain ranges in Utah. The terraces indicate several old shorelines of a huge Pleistocene lake called Lake Bonneville. The Great Salt Lake is a remnant of Lake Bonneville.

↑ The mountains by Great Salt Lake show where several different shorelines existed in the past.

When ice formed again, the Columbia River was dammed once more. A series of floods deeply eroded a large section of eastern Washington. This area is now called the Channeled Scablands. The topsoil was scraped off and the rock was eroded. One of the main features left behind was the Grand Coulee (a coulee is a dry canyon). Today, the Grand Coulee Dam is the largest electricity-making dam in North America.

In the middle of the continent, rivers formed as the ice sheet retreated. That ice prevented the rivers from draining northward. The water backed up, forming a lake that is called Lake Agassiz. It once covered most of Manitoba, Saskatchewan, and Ontario. It also stretched southward into the north-central United States. The lake may have measured 700 miles (1,100 km) by 200 miles (320 km).

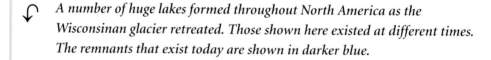

A number of huge lakes formed throughout North America as the Wisconsinan glacier retreated. Those shown here existed at different times. The remnants that exist today are shown in darker blue.

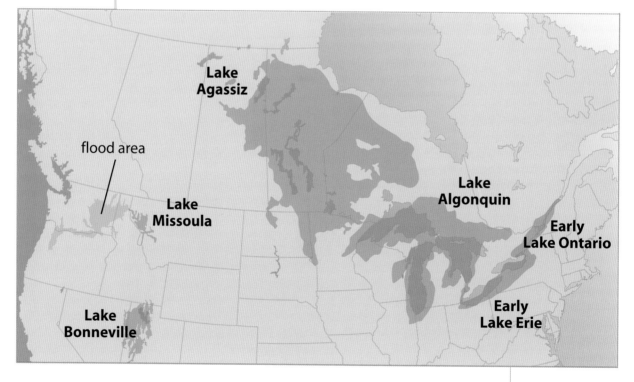

When the ice sheet melted back enough, the lake was finally able to drain into Hudson Bay. It left behind some smaller but spectacular lakes. These include Lake of the Woods and Lake Winnipeg. Lake Agassiz also drained toward the south. It then drained through the valleys of today's Minnesota and Mississippi rivers.

Glacial Lake Agassiz existed for more than 4,000 years. Eventually, it drained away. The lake left behind muds and clays up to 95 feet (29 m) thick. This made the region one of the most fertile in the world. As the lake retreated, forests began to grow where it had existed. Then the forested areas became prairie. About 10,000 years ago, Native Americans moved onto the prairie.

The ice sheets gouged out Hudson Bay itself. The gouging dug a basin in Paleozoic rock. The basin filled with saltwater as the ice sheet retreated. This early version of Hudson Bay is called the Tyrrell Sea. It had a diameter as much as 155 miles (250 km) larger than we see it now.

As ice melted, the land beneath it was lifted up when the restraining weight of the ice went away. The region around Hudson Bay has been rising since the end of the Wisconsin glaciation. It may have risen as much as 400 feet (120 m). It is still rising today. Each century it rises about 20 inches (50 cm). Over thousands of years, this rising land will change the way rivers drain throughout Canada.

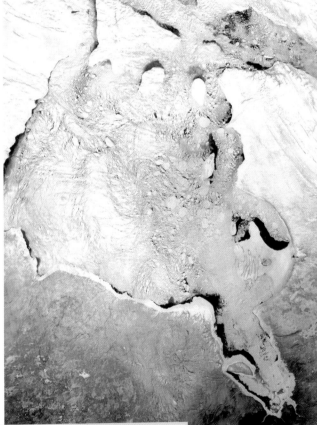

Hudson Bay in northern Canada was gouged out of the surface ↑
by the last glaciation. It is seen here frozen over in winter.

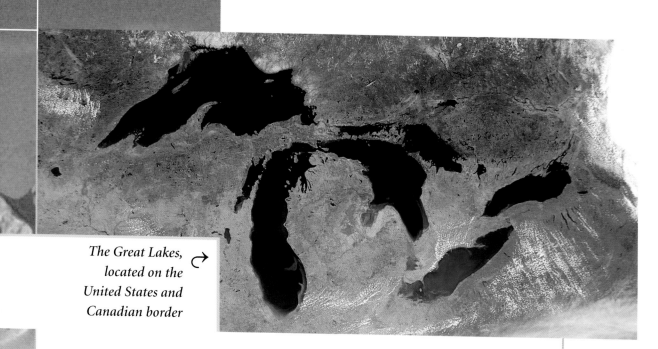

The Great Lakes, located on the United States and Canadian border

The Great Lakes are what remain of a mammoth ancient glacial lake. This lake was called Lake Algonquin. About 11,000 years ago, much of it drained away. This left the three western lakes, Superior, Michigan, and Huron. Much of the drainage was to the east. Water there backed up into another ancient lake. This lake was called Iroquois. It filled Lake Ontario. Lake Ontario then filled Lake Erie. Lake Erie formed within a depression that had originally been a river. The Great Lakes now drain to the Atlantic Ocean through the St. Lawrence River.

Each time ice sheets formed, they destroyed the previous drainage systems in the areas they covered. Before the Ice Age, most of the rivers of the northern United States and Canada drained northward. They drained into the region now occupied by Hudson Bay. But the ice sheets destroyed that system. Now, most of the rivers in central North America flow toward the Mississippi River.

A Special Kind of Lake

Glaciers were not the only force at work during the Pleistocene. Away from the glacial area itself, other lakes formed. This occurred because areas that are now fairly dry got a great deal of rain. This rain was a side effect of the lowered temperature.

One of the most amazing of these special lakes was Lake Bonneville. This huge lake existed for about 15,000 years, until about 14,000 years ago. When it was at its largest, the lake was 325 miles (523 km) long and 135 miles (217 km) wide. It may have been 1,100 feet (335 m) deep. It covered about 20,000 square miles (5,180 sq km) in Nevada, Utah, and Idaho. Islands within the lake are now exposed as mountains.

Bonneville was a terminal lake. This means that no rivers flowed from it. The lake existed in what is now called the Great Basin. This is an entire region into which rivers flow but do not come out. The Great Basin covers an area of about 200,000 square miles (518,000 sq km). The water does not come out of the Great Basin to make its way out to the ocean, as most water does. Because the water doesn't escape, it evaporates. This leaves behind crystals of the minerals it contains.

Over time, ancient Lake Bonneville gradually shrank. The crust beneath the ancient lake has risen because of the loss of water weight on it. As the lake shrank, old shorelines left terraces on the surrounding mountains. The final remnant of Lake Bonneville is Great Salt Lake in Utah.

Many features of North America were formed during the Pleistocene, especially by the Wisconsinan glaciation. There are far too many features to describe them all here. Today's residents of the northern half of the continent see land that was formed by the Wisconsinan ice sheet.

When Lake Bonneville disappeared, it left behind a huge flat area of crystals (salt). The ancient lake has been used for speed trials for land vehicles. This is because Bonneville Salt Flats are so smooth.

Ice Age Life

Chapter 4

The ice sheets of the Pleistocene were limited to the northern parts of the continent. Their presence, however, affected living things throughout North America and even Asia.

The ice sheets expanded southward. As a result, many plants and animals lost their familiar habitats. Some species were able to move south. Others became **extinct**. The Wisconsinan ice sheet reached down into southern Illinois.

The area adjacent to, or neighboring, the front of the ice sheet, from the North Atlantic west, became permafrost. The ground underneath was permanently frozen. However, the upper layer would melt during the summer. It then would become marshy land that supported a little plant growth. Such a habitat is called tundra. It exists today around the Arctic Ocean. Twenty thousand years ago, however, tundra could be found all the way south into northern Kentucky.

Woolly mammoths and the shaggy-haired musk oxen were among the big mammals that inhabited the Pleistocene tundra. Today, the elephantlike mammoth is gone, but the musk oxen still live in the far north. They are shown on the title page of this book.

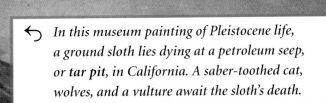

In this museum painting of Pleistocene life, a ground sloth lies dying at a petroleum seep, or tar pit, in California. A saber-toothed cat, wolves, and a vulture await the sloth's death.

Tundra was the typical habitat of the continental shelf. The shelf was exposed between northern North America and Asia. For thousands of years, this land, called Beringia, was the homeland of many animals. They came both from North America and from Asia. Among these animals were mammoths, mastodons, musk oxen, cave lions, and wild horses. Also making the trek to North America from Asia was the ancestor of the bison.

South of the tundra there were evergreen **conifer** forests, especially spruce. These trees occupied the central portion of what became the United States. Conifers had already occupied the west. They continue to do so today.

The Land Without Snakes

Tundra covered the exposed continental shelf between the European continent and Great Britain. It's a famous fact that Ireland has no snakes. This is despite the fact that Ireland is only a few miles off the coast of Great Britain, which does have snakes. This phenomenon occurred because the only connection between the two islands was a land bridge. This bridge formed during the last Ice Age. It was extremely cold at that time. Reptiles could not survive the cold while crossing the land bridge. Eventually, the climate began to warm up. The sea level rose. The land bridge disappeared about 12,000 years ago. It then was too late for most reptiles to make it to Ireland.

Farther south, there were hardwood deciduous (leaf-shedding) forests. These occupied the Coastal Plain along the Gulf of Mexico. Today, they are the primary forests of much of eastern North America. They no longer exist in large numbers along the Coastal Plain.

The land that became the southern United States was getting plenty of rain. At the same time, the rain forests along the equator were getting very little. Equatorial forests shrank during the Ice Age.

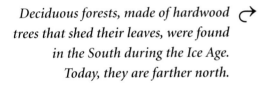

Deciduous forests, made of hardwood ↱
trees that shed their leaves, were found
in the South during the Ice Age.
Today, they are farther north.

Large Mammals

Many of the mammals that occupied Beringia (as well as much of ice-free North America) were large. They are often referred to as **megafauna**, meaning "extra-large animals." As the temperatures cooled during the Tertiary Period, some mammals grew larger. A large mammal retains body heat longer than a small one does. There is less surface area through which heat is lost in proportion to the animal's size. Their size gave these Ice Age mammals an advantage. But, as we'll see, this advantage did not last.

↰ A North American mastodon

Looking at Mammoths and Mastodons

Most tall animals have long necks. Such a neck enables them to reach the ground to feed and drink. Elephants and their ancient relatives, the mammoths and mastodons, have short, muscular necks. They need these to support their large heads. But they can still reach the ground. They use a long trunk, or proboscis to carry food and water to the mouth.

Mastodons were the first of these animals to evolve. They occupied North America as early as 20 million years ago. They were probably browsing animals. They had teeth designed for grinding leaves. A mastodon's jaws were long. Like modern elephants, they developed tusks. Some had tusks in both the upper and lower jaws. One had tusks that curved backward toward its body. Mastodons were rarely more than 10 feet (3 m) tall.

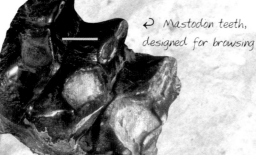

↰ Mastodon teeth, designed for browsing

A mammoth tooth, ↱ designed for grazing

↑ A woolly mammoth and skeleton

Mammoths did not come to North America until well into the Pleistocene. That was about 1.6 million years ago. Some of them were much taller than mastodons. They often had long hair, sometimes 3 feet (0.9 m) long. They had teeth with rough points. These helped them chew up food that was much coarser than mastodons ate. They used their 10-foot (3-m) tusks to scrape through ice in their tundra habitat and reach the grasses beneath. Humans knew the woolly mammoths. They probably worked in groups to hunt the big beasts.

During the Pleistocene, mastodons and true elephants were very common in North America. Mammoths were not so common. However, complete skeletons of mammoths are found in most large museums. An unusually large concentration of their remains is found at a site in Hot Springs, South Dakota.

↶ A mammoth bone bed at Hot Springs

The largest species of mammoth has been called the imperial mammoth. It stood more than 14 feet (4.2 m) tall at the shoulders. It was an animal of the grasslands. The imperial mammoth lived almost entirely on grasses. It had tusks that curved upward and back. Its tusks could be 15 feet (4.8 m) long.

The giant beaver was about 8 feet (2.5 m) long. It weighed about 450 pounds (204 kg). This bear-sized herbivore lived from Florida up into the Yukon, depending on where the ice sheet was. Today's small beaver lived at the same time and in the same places as its giant relative.

The most famous petroleum seep, or tar pit, in the world is one on Rancho La Brea in Los Angeles. Millions of fossils have been found preserved in the black ooze.

The Tar Pit Museum

Asphalt is a thick, black petroleum material. It has seeped through layers of sedimentary rock up onto the surface of southern California for perhaps 40,000 years. It gathered in depressions called tar pits. These areas appeared to be normal ground, so animals often walked across them. But the animals were caught in the sticky tar, and there they died. They were often killed and eaten by waiting predators. Their bones were rapidly buried in the asphalt. They could not disintegrate there because there was no oxygen. Instead, they became fossilized by absorbing the petroleum.

↖ *Bones found in the tar were fossilized by the absorption of petroleum.*

Tar Pits of Rancho La Brea

The La Brea tar pits are located in downtown Los Angeles. The Page Museum is at the site. The museum displays a collection of Ice Age fossils.

During the Pleistocene, animals became trapped in the sticky, heavy oils of the petroleum pools. An unusually large percentage of the fossils found at the pools are those of carnivores and scavengers. They were probably at the pools trying to take advantage of any trapped plant-eaters. The most common fossil found is the dire wolf. It was not much larger than today's gray wolf. However, it could crush the bones of much larger bison with its powerful jaws.

Pools of asphalt still form. They are not as large as they would have been during the Pleistocene, however. The climate of that area must have been similar to what it is today because the types of fossils found at the pools are similar to modern wildlife in the area.

↓ *Dire wolf skeletons*

↗ *A Pleistocene beetle*

The smilodon, or the saber-toothed cat, appeared in the fossil record about 1.6 million years ago. (The smilodon is sometimes called the saber-toothed tiger, although it is not especially related to today's tiger.) We think of the carnivores we know with large tusklike teeth as being able to eat anything they caught. The smilodon's sword-shaped teeth were quite fragile, however. They broke easily if they accidentally munched bone.

Smilodons were about the size of today's lions. They weighed perhaps 600 pounds (273 kg). Their fossils were found throughout North America south of the tundra line.

↩ *The smilodon, or saber-toothed cat, lived until about 11,000 years ago throughout North America south of the tundra line. Humans probably played a role in its extinction.*

Some mammals came into North America from South America. This occurred after the Isthmus of Panama closed the connection between the two continents. Giant camels had come to North America from Asia. By the time they made their way down into South America across the Isthmus, they were already small. Today, there are four small South American camels. Camels are now extinct in North America.

The giant ground sloth, or *Megatherium*, lived in Florida and over into Texas during the Pleistocene. It was even larger than today's elephants. Today, its relatives are South American tree sloths, which are quite small.

The migrating animals weren't necessarily large. The opossum is an example. It is the only marsupial (pouched mammal) that has made its

↱ *The* Glyptodon, *or giant armadillo, has been described as being the size of a car. A giant ground sloth stands in the background.*

way back into North America. It has even been found as far north as some places in Canada along the border with the United States.

Several species of giant armadillo, or *Glyptodon*, also reached North America across the Isthmus. These were large, heavily armored mammals. They occupied Mexico and the coast of the Gulf of Mexico.

The cave bear was considerably larger ↱ *than its modern equal, the brown bear. It shared its existence with the humans spreading out through North America.*

Giant Birds

It wasn't only the mammals that were huge when the Quaternary started. As recently as 1.8 million years ago, a giant predatory bird occupied the southern states. It came from South America across the new Isthmus of Panama. It was called *Titanis*, meaning "terror bird." This bird was flightless but ran very swiftly. It was vicious in its attack on other animals. Instead of wings, it had powerful arms and clawed hands. *Teratornis* (left) was found in the La Brea Tar Pits. It was a coastal predator with a wingspan of 14 feet (4.3 m).

The Coming of Humans

A small section of the Yukon Territory, adjacent to Alaska, was not glaciated. This may have been because the climate was too dry. Not enough snow fell to form glacial ice. This ice-free area may have formed an actual corridor along the Rocky Mountains. The corridor reached down into what is now the United States.

Human beings crossed Beringia at any time during the last 100,000 years. The humans that reached North America and traveled the ice-free corridor southward were not ancestral humanoid species, such as Australopithecines. Hunter-gatherers, they were the modern *Homo sapiens*, meaning "wise man." Archaeologists have evidence of them living here at least 30,000 years ago.

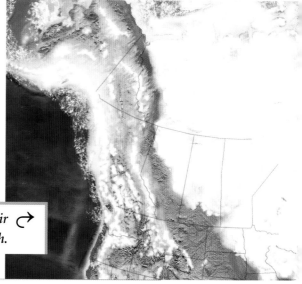

Migrating humans from Asia may have found their way into North America by an ice-free path. ⟳

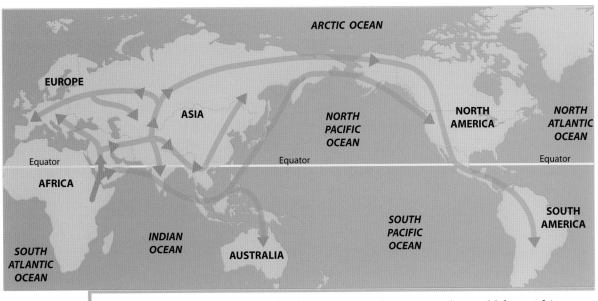

↺ *Scientists have proposed that humans spread out across the world from Africa.*

No one is certain when humans arrived in North America from Asia. Traditionally, scientists have assumed that it was after the last ice sheet melted. However, they are now finding out that humans spread from Africa throughout the different continents more rapidly than previously thought. There is also evidence now that some humans may have arrived in North America by boat at an earlier time.

Archaeologists at work in Colorado ↱
digging up evidence of a Native
civilization from 8800 B.C.

↺ *An artist's view of what a struggle between humans and mastodons might have been like. Hunters worked together to bring down the big beasts. Sophisticated flint weapons, like that below, did not come into use until later.*

The Pleistocene Extinctions

About 10,000 years ago, the megafauna of North America died out. This occurred at the start of the Holocene. As often happens, scientists argue about why that dramatic extinction occurred. Elsewhere in the world, Pleistocene extinctions also took place. However, these extinctions did not cause nearly such great loss as in North America.

For a long time, it was assumed that these extinctions were caused by climate change. Sea level may have risen and fallen as many as twenty times during the Pleistocene. The climate would have changed that often, too. Only living things that can handle great changes in climate can survive such ups and downs. Many large mammals could not handle those changes. As a result, they became extinct.

Climate changes were not new to these large mammals, however. They had survived the many ice sheets of the Pleistocene. Why did they not survive better weather? Perhaps they could not survive the change from spruce forests to deciduous forests as the ice sheet retreated. Or perhaps there was a serious disease that destroyed the giant beasts.

In recent years, scientists have generally come to accept another idea. They believe that human beings killed off the megafauna of North America. During the late Pleistocene, large mammals of all continents except Africa became extinct. Human beings expanded into new territories at the same time. These extinctions followed that expansion. The large animals were generally slow moving. They could not compete with the weapons the humans developed.

Whatever the cause, the big mammals and birds that inhabited North America were gone. The living things we know today are basically the ones that were left when the Holocene began 10,000 years ago.

The North American peccary, a wild pig, lived during the Pleistocene. Peccaries hunted in vicious packs, but humans were able to destroy the species. ↰

Chapter 5

The Holocene:
The Age of Humans

A new epoch in Earth's history began about 10,000 years ago. This was when the last ice sheet melted back into the Arctic. That has been a short time period in geologic time. It is not yet possible to define the Holocene Epoch geologically. And yet, change continues to happen. We'll take a look at two examples: Chesapeake Bay on the eastern shore of the United States, and the Great Plains, which occupy the central part of both Canada and the United States.

Chesapeake Bay

During the Quaternary, the eastern shore of North America alternately widened and narrowed. This happened as sea level dropped and then rose. Throughout all this period, rivers of many sizes carried sediment to the area. This built up the Coastal Plain.

Chesapeake Bay is the largest **estuary** in North America. An estuary is a section of a river in which saltwater from the ocean and freshwater from the continent mix. An estuary has a very different kind of environment than either the ocean or the rivers.

By the time the last ice sheet melted back, humans were already living in the Chesapeake region. The melting ice sent water into the bay. This water came from more than 50 rivers and their tributaries. It wasn't until about 4,000 years ago that the bay took on the shape we know today. However, even that shape continues to change in many ways.

↱ *Shorelines on Chesapeake Bay change as water levels change.*

↰ *Humans came to North America only about 30,000 years ago, but now we can see our continent, and our world, from space. This space photo shows central Illinois, where the Lewis and Clark Expedition was made ready to explore the West in 1804.*

The water within the bay is rising at twice the speed of the main sea level. Rising tides eat away at the shore on both sides of the bay. They are also gradually submerging many of the islands in the bay. The shape of Chesapeake Bay will continue to change.

The North American Great Plains have ↱ *been called the "breadbasket of the world" because so much grain is grown.*

The Great Plains

The Great Plains cover the southern parts of Alberta, Saskatchewan, and Manitoba in Canada. They continue through all or part of twelve states, down to Texas. The region is significant because of the crops that grow in fertile soil. The soil was deposited by the meltwaters of the last ice sheet. These crops feed a large percentage of the human population of the world. They grow despite the fact that the Great Plains are fairly dry. They are dry enough to support only a few trees. Crops must be heavily irrigated.

During the Eocene Period, the region turned into grasslands. This occurred more than 50 million years ago. The region was the primary home for all the hoofed animals that developed in North America.

Bison, or American buffalo, inhabited the grasslands of the Great Plains. They served as a primary food for the humans that spread across the plains.

The climate cooled leading into the Pleistocene. As it cooled, northern spruce forests grew up. They were followed by deciduous forests until about 6,000 years ago. At that time, the grasslands returned. Ancient American Indians were already hunting bison across the Plains. They hunted on foot, however.

Change on the Great Plains has not stopped. Scientists in southern Canada have found evidence of a severe drought. This occurred during the last 10,000 years. The flourishing grasslands habitat has often suffered from drought. During long periods of drought, sands have formed into dunes. These sands were originally dropped by the ice sheets. The sands spread out again, and then formed more dunes.

The period called the Great Drought occurred as recently as about A.D. 1275. It devastated much of western North America. This was probably when some great Native American civilizations such as the Anazasi disappeared.

The Anasazi were probably driven from their cave homes by drought.

Geologic Change Continues

Each of us lives perhaps 70 to 100 years. This time seems pleasantly long, taken day by day. We rarely see the kind of gelogic activity that has created the earth as we know it. Most of it is far too slow for us to see or feel. Only the most sophisticated instruments record this activity. But Earth's crust can also change suddenly. Earthquakes continue to take place.

At the end of 2004, an earthquake took place in the seafloor of the Indian Ocean off the coast of Indonesia. It may have been the second-most powerful earthquake ever recorded. The movement of the seafloor set off a huge wave, called a **tsunami**. It moved with incredible speed and power over the coastal regions of eleven countries, north to India and west to Africa. In all, probably a quarter of a million people were killed. Whole communities disappeared.

This is only one small part of the Indian Ocean islands that were wiped clean by the tsunami of 2004. Only an Islamic mosque was left standing in this part of Sumatra.

Volcanoes, too, are not just prehistoric events. Along the southern margin of the Colorado Plateau in Arizona is an area called the San Francisco Volcanic Field. For 6 million years, volcanoes have been erupting in the area. There are perhaps 600 of them. This volcanic field was created by the magma that lifted the Colorado Plateau.

Native Americans living in the northern Arizona area in A.D. 1064 witnessed a huge volcanic event. They must have been horrified to see fiery rocks exploding out of the ground. Before the eruption stopped, a new volcanic mountain had been formed. It was about 1,000 feet (330 m) high.

Arizona's Sunset Crater is a cinder cone formed in the San Francisco Volcanic Field. When it erupted a thousand years ago, it drove many Native Americans from their homes.

Today, the rough lava still looks as if it had just cooled. Multicolored minerals settled around the top of the vent. These gave the volcano the name Sunset Crater.

Geologists think that the hot spot creating the San Francisco Volcanic Field is still there. New volcanoes could erupt in the region in the future.

The Cascade Range runs from central California up into British Columbia. It has had a great deal of volcanic activity during the last 2 million years. This occurs because the small Juan de Fuca tectonic plate is **subducting** (being drawn down) under the North America plate. As a result, volcanoes form inland on the continental crust.

The most recent major eruption in the Cascades was the explosion of Mount St. Helens in Washington State. Starting on March 20, 1980, geologists recorded earthquake activity in the region. The rumbling increased day by day. Geologists knew an eruption was likely to take place. On May 18, the north side of the mountain blew out.

The forest surrounding Mount St. Helens was blown completely down for 19 miles (30 km) on May 18, 1980. Sixty people were killed by the eruption.

Before

The Mount St. Helens Eruption

Mount St. Helens is about 40,000 years old. It is part of the Cascade Range. This range also includes such well-known peaks as Mounts Rainier, Hood, and Shasta. These volcanic peaks are often referred to as composite volcanoes. This is because they are built up by layers of lava flows. They are also composed of material that has been thrown outward by explosive forces. Such volcanoes can be destructive.

Mount St. Helens had been dormant since 1857. It started rumbling again in 1980. The violent eruption blew out one face of the mountain, revealing its crater. During later, smaller eruptions, a lava dome formed from lava that was too thick to flow from the vent. The dome can be seen inside the crater.

During

After

The mountain is now monitored for signs of another eruption. In 2004, the mountain started rumbling again. The volcano released steam and gases. The lava dome inside the crater continued to build up. Sightseers were kept several miles from the volcano.

Climate Change

The Ice Age is not over. Today's ice sheets in the Northern Hemisphere still cover Greenland, northern Canada, and Baffin Island. In the south, a vast ice sheet covers Antarctica. Altogether, about 5 percent of Earth's surface is still covered in ice.

There is still plenty of freshwater locked up in ice sheets. There is more freshwater stored in ice than in all the world's lakes, rivers, and the atmosphere combined. Today's ice sheets have been estimated as occupying 25 million cubic kilometers. That is a full third of the amount of space they occupied at the height of the Ice Age.

Scientists challenge each other on ideas about climate change. They discuss whether climate change brought about the ice sheets, or whether the presence of the ice sheets changed the climate. Of course, both ideas must ask what brought about the ice sheets or the climate change in the first place. There is still plenty of room for discoveries and new ideas.

The existence of human beings may be a significant factor in any climate change of the future. Human activities contributed to many of the changes taking place in the landscape of North America. For example, dams make new lakes, mountainsides are sheared away for development, freshwater supplies are used up—all as a result of human activity.

↩ *Peat beds in Canada can provide both fuel and special soils used in planting flowers.*

Humans have the ability to take advantage of natural resources of the planet. This is unlike any other animal. The resources have developed over millions of years. We use the rock formed long ago to build structures and to keep warm.

We think of **coal** as a rock that formed a very long time ago. And yet **peat** is still being formed, and peat is the first stage in coal production. It forms when vegetable matter dies and falls into water that doesn't drain away. As a result, the matter partially rots. When dried, peat can be used as a fuel. About 12 percent of Canada's land consists of peat. It formed during the Quaternary. This is the largest supply of peat in the world.

Oil from Rock

A region of northeastern Alberta contains a special kind of rock called Athabascan tar sands. This gluey, sandy clay may be the world's next source of petroleum. Some estimates say that there are perhaps a trillion and a half barrels of oil. But it's not in neat pockets that can be drilled and pumped. Instead, the oil has to be processed out of the **shale** rock. It will be very expensive to mine this oil. Even so, the cost of Arabian oil is getting quite high. As a result, oil companies are looking to Canada for the next source of oil.

The Rocky Mountains in Colorado, Utah, and Wyoming have similar oil shale. During the 1980s, several petroleum companies did some work on producing oil from the rock. So far, none has stayed with the project,

Seattle, Washington, seen here at dusk, lies only a few miles from Mount Rainier in the Cascade Range. It has been 150 years since Mount Rainier erupted, but many geologists think that it might erupt again.

The Future

Today, we live in a comparatively warm interglacial period. It is possible that ice sheets will start building up again. This may happen perhaps in about 5,000 years. However, humans have made geological changes on Earth that might make things different this time around. By burning **fossil fuels** (coal, oil, and natural gas), we have dumped huge amounts of carbon dioxide (CO_2) into the atmosphere. As we've seen, CO_2 holds solar heat in the atmosphere. This raises the temperature of the planet.

Perhaps our interglacial is going to get much warmer than the previous warm periods. If so, the ice sheets covering Greenland and Antarctica might melt. Sea level could rise as much as 160 feet (50 m). If that were to happen, vast areas of the continents close to the oceans could be flooded. And those are the areas where most people live.

Many scientists are studying **global warming**. It is clear that humans have played a major role in warming the planet. However, there appear to be many other factors that we know little about. These factors could also play a role in global temperature change and how to solve it.

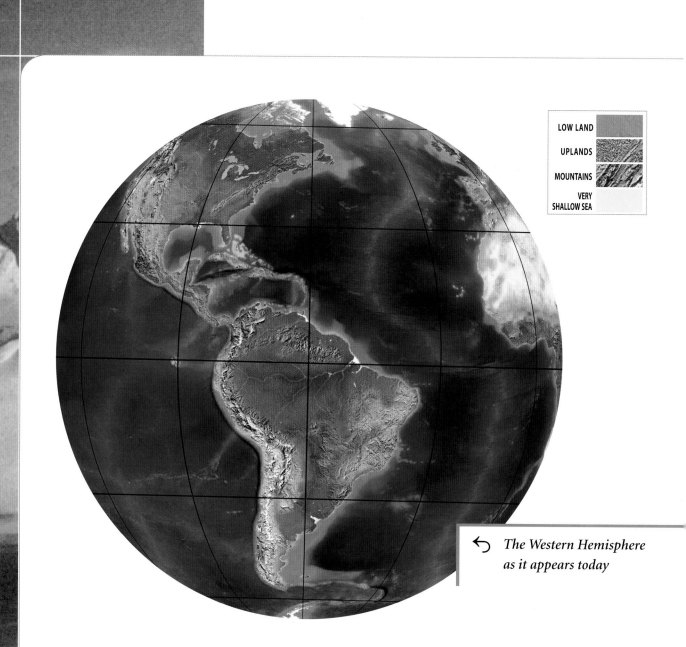

LOW LAND	
UPLANDS	
MOUNTAINS	
VERY SHALLOW SEA	

↶ *The Western Hemisphere as it appears today*

Earth has existed for at least 4.6 billion years. The continent now called North America has existed for perhaps two-thirds of that time. North America has moved around on a tectonic plate during those 3 billion or more years. The plate on which it rides has been pushed and pulled by forces within the earth.

The land that we know, however, has existed only during the last few million years. It could change tomorrow, through earthquakes, volcanoes, or even the collision of an object from outer space. But it probably won't.

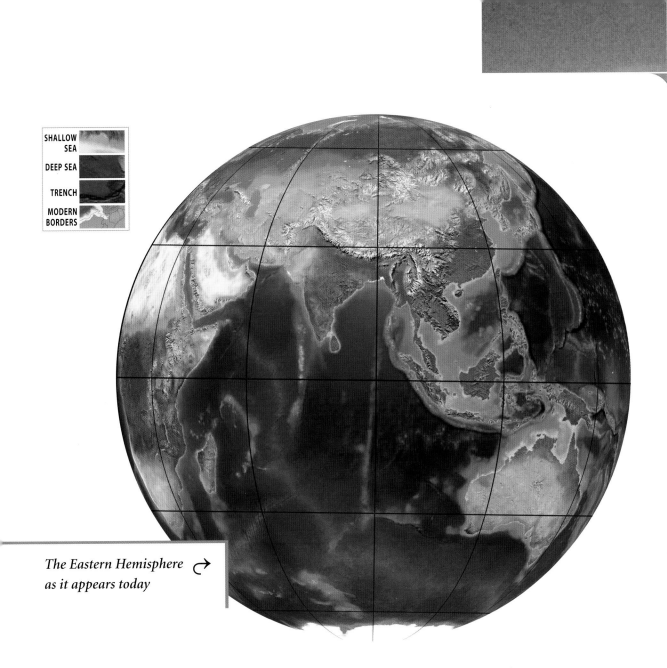

SHALLOW SEA
DEEP SEA
TRENCH
MODERN BORDERS

The Eastern Hemisphere ⤳
as it appears today

The processes that change our continent, and the entire planet, tend to take place very slowly.

The biggest change in the last few million years has been the evolution of human beings. North America is still moving westward at a rate of about 31 miles (50 km) every million years. We are the only creatures on the planet that are able to realize this. We are also the only creatures who might cause events—deliberately or not—that could change the way our planet will look in the future.

GEOLOGIC TIME SCALE

PRECAMBRIAN TIME • 4.5 billion to 543 million years ago

Time Period	Tectonic Events	Biological Events
Hadean Eon *4.5–3.96 billion years ago* Named for Hades, or Hell	No Earth rocks from this time found	None
Archean Eon *3.96–2.5 billion years ago* Name means "Ancient"	Oldest known rocks First permanent crust First stable continents	Seawater formed First bacteria Atmosphere formed
Proterozoic Eon *2.5 billion–543 million*	North American craton formed First iron–bearing sediments First large glaciation Formation and breakup of Rodinia supercontinent Gondwana, southern supercontinent, formed	Free oxygen in atmosphere First nucleated cells, allowing sexual reproduction First multicellular animals First animals with exoskeletons First fungi

PHANEROZOIC TIME • 543 million years ago to present

PALEOZOIC ERA • 543 to 248 million years ago

Time Period	Tectonic Events	Biological Events
Cambrian Period *543–248 million years ago* Named for old name of Wales	Laurentia separated from Siberia	Cambrian Explosion: Major diversification of marine invertebrates
Ordovician Period *490–443 million years ago* Named for a Celtic tribe in Wales	First Iapetus Ocean Taconic orogeny in northeastern Laurentia	First true vertebrates: jawless fish First land plants Mass extinction
Silurian Period *443–417 million years ago* Named for a Celtic tribe in Wales	Caledonian orogeny Shallow seas on Laurentia	First vascular plants First insects First jawed fish
Devonian Period *417–354 million years ago* Named for Devon, England	Major reef building	First forests First seed–baring plants First four–footed animals First amphibians
CARBONIFEROUS PERIOD *354 to 290 million years ago* — **Mississippian Epoch** *354–323 million years ago* Named for Mississippi River Valley	Antler orogeny	Ferns abundant First land vertebrates
Pennsylvanian Epoch *323–290 million years ago* Named for coal formations in Pennsylvania	Appalachian orogeny began Antler orogeny	Ferns abundant Major coal–forming forests First reptiles
Permian *290–248 million years ago* Named for Russian province of Perm	Pangea formed	First warm–blooded reptiles Greatest mass extinction

MESOZOIC ERA
248 to 65 million years ago

Time Period	Tectonic Events	Biological Events
Triassic Period *248–206 million years ago* Named for three layers in certain European rocks	Pangea completed Major part of Pangea was arid	First flying vertebrates First dinosaurs First mammals Cephalopods abundant
Jurassic Period *206–144 million hears ago* Named for the Jura Mountains	Atlantic began to open Pangea separated into Gondwana and Laurasia	First birds Cycads abundant
Cretaceous Period *144–65 million years ago* Named after Latin word for " chalk"	Major volcanism Sevier orogeny Laurentia separated from Eurasia Sierra Nevada batholith	First flowering plants First social insects Mass extinction of dinosaurs

CENOZOIC ERA • 65 million years ago to present

TERTIARY PERIOD • 65 to 1.8 million years ago

Time Period	Tectonic Events	Biological Events
Paleocene Epoch *65 to 54.8 million years ago*	Laramide orogeny Western Laurentia uplifted	Mammals and birds diversified First horse ancestors
Eocene Epoch *54.8 to 33.7 million years ago*	Rockies uplifted Global cooling began	First mammals (whales) in sea First primates First cats and dogs
Oligocene Epoch *33.7 to 23.8 million years ago*	North Atlantic opened Ice cap formed in Anatarctica	First apes Grasslands widespread
Miocene Epoch *23.8 to 5.3 million years ago*	Columbia flood basalts	First human ancestors First mastodons
Pliocene Epoch *5.3 to 1.8 million years ago*	Northern Hemisphere glaciation began Cascade Volcanoes	Large mammals abundant

QUATERNARY PERIOD • 1.8 million to today

Time Period	Tectonic Events	Biological Events
Pleistocene Epoch *1.8 million years ago to today*	Great glaciation of Northern Hemisphere	First modern humans Extinction of large mammals Humans entered North America
Holocene *10,000 years ago to today*	Rifting continued in East Africa Human–caused global warming	Human-caused extinctions

GLOSSARY

asthenosphere the part of Earth's mantle that lies beneath the lithosphere. This zone of soft, easily deformed rock is believed to be less rigid, hotter, and more fluid than the rock above or below.

axis the imaginary pole extending from the North Pole to the South Pole on which Earth turns

basin a low area, or depression, in the earth's surface that collects sediment. In the sea, this depression is cut off from ocean currents. Crystallized mineral deposits collect here and harden into rock.

bedrock the bottom or lowest layer of rock; solid rock tha lies beneath soil and other surface materials

calcium carbonate the mineral $CaCO_3$, which is the principal component of limestone and chalk

caldera a large, basinlike depression that results from the collapse or explosion of the center of an erupting volcano

calving the production of icebergs from a glacier

Canadian Shield the largest area of exposed Precambrian rock on Earth. This ancient rock of the North American craton covers more than 1.8 million square miles (4.8 million sq km) from the Great Lakes to the Canadian Arctic to Greenland.

cinder cone a steep, cone-shaped volcano formed by lightweight, gas-filled lava; may exist on its own or may form around a vent on the side of another volcano

coal sedimentary rock derived from partially decomposed, carbonized plant matter. This black or dark brown mineral substance is used as fuel.

Coastal Plain a generally flat area of sedimentary rock along a seacoast between hard rock and the ocean; When capitalized, it generally refers to the plain along the east and southern coast of the United States. Without capitals, any coastal plain.

coccoliths limestone scales or plates formed by single-celled algae that are part of plankton; the name may be used for both the algae and their scales

conifer a type of tree or shrub that is generally evergreen, has needle-like leaves, and bears its seeds on cones, such as pines

continental shelf the part of a continent that is submerged in a shallow sea, thus forming an underwater shelf. It slopes downward to a depth of 200 meters. Marine life first developed on shelves surrounding the Paleozoic continents.

Cordillera the region of North America made up of the entire chain of mountain ranges parallel to the Pacific Coast, from Mexico to Alaska

core 1) the interior part of Earth beginning at about 1,800 miles (2,900 km) below Earth's surface. Composed mostly of iron and nickel, it is divided into two parts: the outer core, which is mostly liquid, and the inner core, which is solid. 2) a cylindrical sample of rock or ice obtained by a special drill

crater a usually circular depression, either in the top of a volcano or formed by the impact of a meteorite

craton the usually stable, unmovable mass of rock in Earth's crust that forms the basic central mass of a continent

crevasse a large crack that forms in the top of a glacier caused by differences in the movement of the different sections of the glacier

crust outermost, rocky layer of Earth. This low-density layer is about 22 miles (35 kilometers) thick under the continents and 6 mi (10 km) thick under the oceans.

drumlin a long hill formed by a glacier overruning glacial till; it lies lengthwise in the direction of the glacier's flow

epoch division of geological time next shorter than a period

era division of geologic time next smaller than the eon and larger than a period. For example, the Cenozoic Era is in the Phanerozoic Eon and includes the Tertiary Period.

esker a snakelike ridge of glacial till that formed in a tunnel at the base of a glacier

estuary the mouth of a river where it enters the sea; the region in which saltwater and freshwater mix

evaporation change of a liquid into a gas, or vapor

extinction the complete disappearance of a species of plant or animal from the earth

fjord a narrow passageway of the sea between cliffs or tall hills, often reaching deeply inland; generally carved by glaciers

foraminiferans marine protozoans with calcite shell. Also known as forams, they are are found in limestone and in the ooze on the ocean floor.

fossil evidence or trace of animal or plant life of a past geological age. These typically mineralized remains have been preserved in rocks of the earth's crust. These traces include bones and footprints of extinct land animals, such as dinosaurs.

fossil fuel coal, petroleum, or natural gas, so called because each was the result of long-term changes in ancient plants and animals

74

fossilize to become a fossil

fumarole a vent in the ground through which steam or gases escape, usually near a volcano

geologic time scale chart that gives the age of the earth. The time is shown in millions of years, with the oldest at the bottom and the youngest at the top The chart used in this book is on pages 72–73.

geyser a hot spring that sends up jets of hot water and steam into the air intermittently, or at a start-and-stop pace

glacial having to do with glaciers or ice sheets; resulting from or associated with the presence of ice or glaciers in great quantities

glacial till the sediment deposited at the leading edge of a glacier; may contain materials of various sizes, from soil to large rocks

glaciation the process of becoming covered by ice or glaciers. It refers to a period of geological time when global cooling occurred and ice sheets covered large areas of the earth.

glacier a mass of dense ice on land that moves slowly, either by coming down from high mountains or spreading out across land from a central point of accumulation

global warming the concept that human activities are contributing to a rise in the temperature of the entire planet

granite coarse-grained, intrusive igneous rock. Granite is composed of sodium and potassium feldspar primarily, but it is also rich in quartz. Light in color, it is a common rock in North America.

heat plume columns of hot material in the earth's mantle that rises toward the ocean ridge; also called mantle plume

hot spot a site of volcanism that is not located near the boundary of a tectonic plate. The Hawaiian Islands were created by a hot spot over which the Pacific plate moves.

Ice Age span of geologic time during the Pleistocene Epoch when much of the Northern Hemisphere was covered with ice sheets

iceberg a chunk of glacial ice that breaks off a glacier and floats in the ocean

ice sheet a glacier that covers much of a continent; usually one that is at least 19,300 square miles (50,000 sq km) in area

igneous rock rock formed directly from magma (molten rock) when it has cooled and solidified. *Igneous* means "fiery."

interglacial the period of comparative warmth between glaciations

island arc a curved or arc-shaped chain of volcanic islands lying near a continent, formed as a result of subduction, such as the Aleutian Islands in Alaska

isotope a variety of a chemical element, which can vary by the number of neutrons in the nucleus

kettle a circular hole in the ground formed by a chunk of a glacier breaking off and later melting

La Brea tar pits site in Southern California where numerous fossils of mammoths, mastodons, and other animals from the Pleistocene Epoch of about 1.8 million years ago are present

lava fluid, molten rock, or magma, that emerges from a volcano or volcanic vent to the earth's surface. When lava is cooled and solidified, it forms an igneous rock such as basalt.

leading edge the edge of a glacier in the direction it is moving; also called the toe

lithosphere hard outer layer of Earth consisting of the crust and the upper part of Earth's mantle. It is broken up into tectonic plates that "float" on the asthenosphere.

magma molten rock that exists beneath the earth's surface. Molten rock that flows to the surface is called lava.

mantle the thickest part of Earth's interior that lies between the crust and the outer core. Along with the crust, the upper mantle forms the lithosphere, which is broken into the plates of plate tectonics.

megafauna extra-large mammals, especially those of the Cenozoic Era

meltwater the water formed by glacier melting; may run off and form a lake

meteorite mass of matter that has reached the earth from outer space

molten liquified by heat

moraine a pile of rocks, pebbles, and other sediment deposited by the movement of a glacier; may be along the side or at the leading edge

normal fault a fault in which the rock on one side slides down the slope of the rock on the other side. A normal fault is no more common than any other kind of fault.

orbit the usually near-circular path a planet or other object follows through space

Pangea (also written **Pangaea**) supercontinent covering about 25 percent of the earth's surface, taking in North America, South America, and part the Middle East. It comprised all of the earth's landmasses at the end of the Paleozoic Era and lasted about 100 million years.

peat partly decayed plant matter deposited in wet environments, such as a marsh or swamp. Peat is used as fuel and contains more than 50% carbon.

period the time interval in geologic history between an era and an epoch. The Quaternary, which we are still in, is the most recent period of the Cenozoic Era

permafrost permanently frozen subsoil

plankton organisms, such as microscopic algae and protozoa, that passively float or drift within a body of water and provide food for many animals

precession the technical term for the "wobble" that Earth's axis makes in space over time

scouring the clearing of loose sediment from a surface by running water or a glacier

sediment loose, uncemented pieces of rock or minerals carried and deposited by water, air, or ice. Sediment may include eroded sand, dirt particles, debris from living things, and solid materials that form as a result of chemical processes.

sedimentary rock rock composed of sediment. Examples include sandstone and limestone. Sedimentary rock typically forms beds, or layers.

shale finely layered sedimentary rock derived from mud; formed by the consolidation of clay, mud, or silt. About 70% of all of Earth's sedimentary rock is shale.

striations long scratches in rock, especially ones made by the movement of a glacier; they indicate direction in which the glacier moved

subduction the movement of ocean seafloor into an undersea depression or trench where it pushes under a tectonic plate and pulls trench sediments down into the earth's mantle

supercontinent giant landmass formed during the Paleozoic Era and made up of several present-day continents. For example, the ancient supercontinent Gondwana contained South America, Africa, southern Europe, the peninsula of Europe, Australia, and Antarctica.

tar pit a place where petroleum seeps from within the earth to the surface. The most famous tar pit is the one at Rancho La Brea in Los Angeles, California, where numerous fossils have been found.

tectonic plate large section of Earth's lithosphere that "floats" on the asthenosphere and moves independently, sometimes rubbing against other plates, sometimes moving apart

tributary a smaller river or glacier that feeds into a larger one

tsunami a large wave that travels along the surface of the ocean set off by an earthquake; sometimes called a tidal wave, but tsunamis have nothing to do with tides

tundra the region toward the poles where only low-growing plants can survive in the soil that thaws in the summer but remains frozen underneath

FURTHER INFORMATION

ONLINE WEB SITES

Museum of Paleontology
University of California at Berkeley
1101 Valley Life Sciences Building
Berkeley, CA 94720
www.ucmp.berkeley.edu/exhibit/exhibits.html
takes you through major exhibits in geology,
evolution, and the classification of living things
Also produced by UCMP is:
www.paleoportal.org
provides a link to many sites for anyone
interested in paleontology

United States Geological Survey
USGS National Center
12201 Sunrise Valley Drive
Reston, VA 20192
www.usgs.gov/education
The Learning Web introduces numerous topics and
projects related to earth science
Find out what's happening at Mount St. Helens
volcano: http://volcanoes.usgs.gov
or where the earthquakes are:
http://earthquake.usgs.gov

The British Broadcasting Corporation has major coverage of prehistoric life:
http://www.bbc.co.uk

MUSEUMS

Be sure to look for museum web sites. Also, be sure to check university and public
museums in your area; they often have good geology exhibits.

<u>UNITED STATES</u>
American Museum of Natural History
Central Park West at 79th St.
New York, NY 10024
www.amnh.org

Colorado School of Mines Geology Museum
13th and Maple St.
Golden, CO 80401

The Field Museum
1400 S. Lake Shore Drive
Chicago, IL 60605
www.fieldmuseum.org
Look for the online exhibit about Sue, the best
preserved *Tyrannosaurus rex*

University of Michigan Museum of Paleontology
1109 Geddes Ave.,
Ann Arbor, MI 48109
www.paleontology.lsa.umich.edu

Smithsonian National Museum of Natural History
10th St. and Constitution Ave.
Washington, D.C. 20560
www.mnh.si.edu

<u>CANADA</u>
Geological Survey of Canada
Earth Sciences Sector
601 Booth St.
Ottawa, Ontario K1A 0E8, Canada
http://ess.nrcan.gc.ca

Canadian Museum of Nature
240 McLeod St.
Ottawa, Ontario K1P 6P4, Canada
www.nature.ca

Provincial Museum of Alberta
12845 102nd Ave.
Edmonton, Alberta T5N 0M6, Canada
www.prma.edmonton.ab.ca

Manitoba Museum of Man and Nature
190 Rupert Avenue
Winnipeg, Manitoba R3B 0N2, Canada
www.manitobamuseum.mb.ca

Pacific Museum of the Earth
6339 Stores Road
Vancouver, British Columbia V6T 1Z4, Canada
www.eos.ubc.ca

DVDs

Amazing Earth, Artisan Entertainment, 2001

Forces of Nature—Book and DVD, National Geographic, 2004

Living Rock: An Introduction to Earth's Geology, WEA Corp, 2002
Also includes 400 USGS "Fact Sheets" in Adobe Acrobat format, obtainable on computer sytems with a DVD-ROM Drive)

Physical Geography: Geologic Time, TMW/Media Group, 2004

Volcano: Nature's Inferno!, National Geographic, 1997

BOOKS

Anderson, Peter. *A Grand Canyon Journey: Tracing Time in Stone.* A First Book. Danbury, CT: Franklin Watts, 1997.

Ball, Jacqueline. *Earth's History.* Discovery Channel School Science series. Milwaukee, WI: Gareth Stevens Publishing, 2004.

Bonner, Hannah. *When Bugs Were Big : Prehistoric Life in a World Before Dinosaurs.* Washington, DC: National Geographic, 2004.

Castelfranchi, Yuri, and Nico Petrilli. *History of the Earth: Geology, Ecology, and Biology.* Hauppage, NY: Barrons, 2003.

Colson, Mary. *Earth Erupts.* Turbulent Earth series. Chicago: Raintree, 2005.

Colson, Mary. *Shaky Ground.* Turbulent Earth series. Chicago: Raintree, 2005.

Day, Trevor. *DK Guide to Savage Earth: An Earth Shattering Journey of Discovery.* New York: Dorling Kindersley, 2001.

Farndon, John. *How the Earth Works.* Pleasantville, NY: Reader's Digest, 1992.

Hooper, Meredith. *The Pebble in My Pocket: A History of Our Earth.* New York: Viking Books, 1996.

Lambert, David. *The Kingfisher Young People's Book of the Universe.* Boston: Kingfisher, 2001.

Maslin, Mark. *Earthquakes.* Restless Planet series. Chicago: Raintree, 2000.

Maynard, Christopher. *My Book of the Prehistoric World.* Boston: Kingfisher, 2001.

Oxlade, Chris. *The Earth and Beyond.* Chicago: Heinemann Library, 1999.

INDEX